Future Island Adventure

LEVEL 6

Written by: Hawys Morgan
Series Editor: Melanie Williams

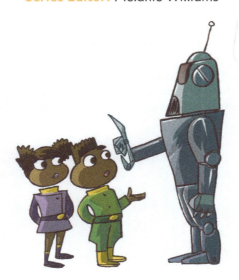

Pearson Education Limited
Edinburgh Gate, Harlow,
Essex CM20 2JE, England
and Associated Companies throughout the world.

ISBN: 978-1-4082-8849-8

This edition first published by Pearson Education Ltd 2014

Eighth impression 2023

Set in 15/19pt OT Fiendstar
Printed by Ashford Colour Press Ltd
SWTC/02

Illustrations: Simone Ermini

For a complete list of the titles available in the Pearson English Kids Readers series, please go to
www.pearsonenglishkidsreaders.com. Alternatively, write to your local Pearson Education office or to
Pearson English Readers Marketing Department, Pearson Education, Edinburgh Gate, Harlow, Essex CM20 2JE, England.

It is one thousand years in the future. One Monday morning on the island of Verdana, a group of children are at school. Leo and Carla, who are twins, go to their history class where they meet their friends, Tim and Ola.

"I hate history," said Leo. "It's boring."

"Shh!" said Carla quietly. "Here comes our teacher, Miss King."

"Good morning, children," said Miss King. "Today, I would like you to do a history project. Please work in groups of four, and find out everything you can about Verdana in the past. Your projects must be ready by next Monday."

The children went on a flying bus to the Verdana City Library.

"This is going to be so boring. Can't we play virtual tennis instead?" said Leo.

"Don't be silly!" laughed Ola. "I think it will be exciting. Let's check the computers in the library."

The only information on the computers was from one hundred years ago. "That's strange. What about history before the robots?" said Carla. "Let's look at some books instead."

Leo asked the robots politely for some books. They rudely replied, "Never!" They looked angry and fierce. "I think we should go!" said Tim.

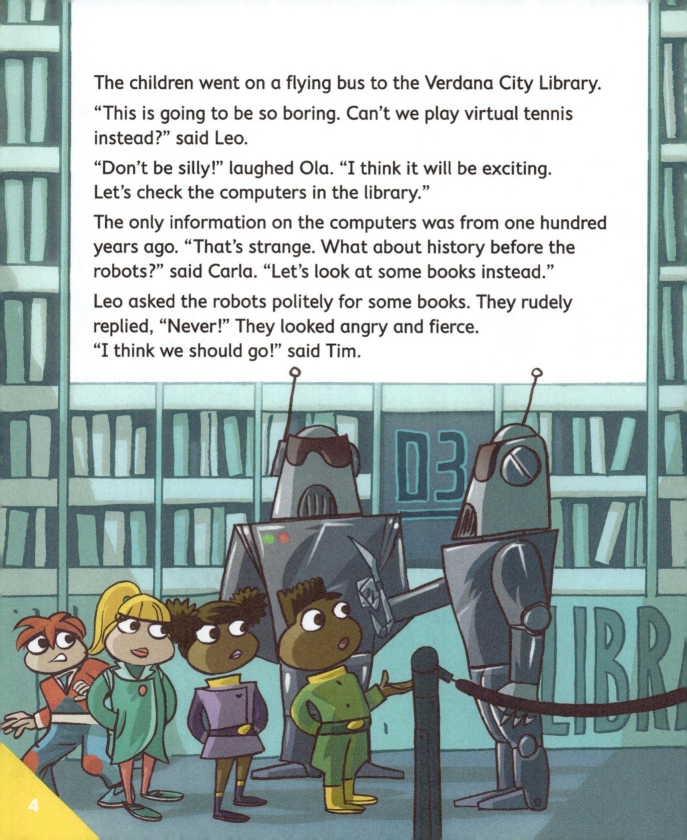

Next, the children went to the museum. In the museum the children saw a plastic cow and a sheep and collections of other extinct Verdanan animals and plants from the past.

Ola noticed that two birds were moving. "Look!" she shouted excitedly. "Real birds! They're not robots!"

They were singing and flying around two plastic birds in an artificial tree, but the museum birds refused to answer.

"Oh no, robots! The robots haven't seen real birds before," Tim said. "They might try to catch them. Robots' hands have sharp metal fingers. Let's get them out of here quickly!"

5

The children ran as fast as they could through the smelly traffic. Dirty cars, buses, and taxis raced over them. The robots followed them through the virtual park, screaming angrily, "STOP! BAD CHILDREN! STOP!"

The robots were very close. The children could hear their metal feet hitting the path. "GIVE US THE ANIMALS!"

Leo noticed a narrow gate. "Hurry!" he shouted. The children kicked away the garbage and escaped through the gate. It was too narrow for the robots, but the children still locked the gate. Then they ran across the bridge over the oily polluted river.

Afterwards, at Ola and Tim's house, Ola brought the birds out of her coat. The children could not stop looking at them.

Tim started laughing. "I can't believe it!" he said. "They're alive – they're not robots! We rescued them."

"Feel their feathers, they are so soft and colorful. Let's call them Rosy and Bluey. Hello Rosy! Hello Bluey," said Leo.

"Hello, goodbye, hello, goodbye," replied the birds. They sang a beautiful song and flew around the room.

"What funny birds!" laughed Tim.

"Why are their feet black?" asked Leo.

"It looks like oil," replied Ola. "Poor birds."

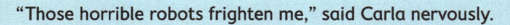

"Those horrible robots frighten me," said Carla nervously.

"We should stay away from them," Tim said. "Our grandfather believes that the computers inside them have gone wrong."

"You should meet our grandfather. He's very interesting," said Ola.

"What's his job?" Leo asked.

"He doesn't work now, but he was a famous plant scientist, explorer, writer, and artist. He's about a hundred and thirty."

"A hundred and thirty? Then he might know more about Verdana's past," said Leo.

"Good idea," said Tim. "I'm worried about grandfather. He never smiles, he always looks sad. He might like the birds."

"We've brought new friends to meet you," Ola called to her grandfather.

"Hello. I'm Leo and this is my sister, Carla," said Leo.

"Welcome," said the old man. "I'm Jon Wiseman, but call me Popp."

Then Popp saw Rosy and Bluey.

"Real birds!" he said. "Do they sing?"

The birds understood and began to sing.

"What wonderful birds!" Popp said, and he smiled for the first time in many years.

The twins looked around the living room at pictures on the walls and books on the shelves.

"Popp painted the pictures," Ola said proudly. "And he wrote the books."

"Tell us about the past, Popp, for our history project," Tim said.

"When I was young," Popp began, "children played on real grass, climbed real trees, and walked in real forests. Birdsong filled the air. Insects and animals were everywhere. Now there's nothing left. Life is sad and boring."

"It's not so bad," said Ola. "We don't miss things we haven't got. We enjoy playing virtual games. I'm good at virtual tennis – *and* real tennis!"

"Well, I like playing virtual football, but it would be fun to play football on real grass," said Tim. "And I'd like a real pet."

"I had a real pet once – a dog called Tag. We played football together on real grass," said Popp.

"Do you have any pictures?" Tim asked.

"Look in my notebooks. I drew Tag once," said Popp.

Popp's notebooks were full of interesting drawings.

"That's Tag," said Popp. "On that perfect day, Tag was trying to catch butterflies and I was collecting plants. It was before Verdana lost its wildlife."

"What do you mean?" Carla asked. "How did Verdana lose its wildlife?"

"I don't like talking about it," Popp replied sadly. "But something terrible happened one day a long time ago."

The children really wanted Popp to tell them how Verdana lost its wildlife.

"It was long ago so it's difficult to remember," said Popp. "But you can look in my notebooks."

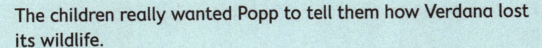

Tim found a page with a dirty black mark and numbers at the top. There were drawings of plants and two strange shapes.

"What are these drawings?" Tim asked. "And what's the black mark?"

"I don't know. I can't remember," said Popp.

"If Rosy and Bluey sing to you, you might remember," said Leo.

"I'll try," Popp replied.

The birds started singing, and then Popp closed his eyes.

"In my mind I see underground caves and a shining lake," Popp said. "I see the entrance to a beautiful forest. I see stalactites and rocks." Then Popp fell asleep.

"The drawings are stalactites!" said Carla. "But what do the numbers mean? And what's the black mark?"

"The mark's a mystery," said Tim. "The numbers could be a date – March the third, three thousand and twenty."

"A hundred years ago!" said Ola. "If we go to the library again, we might find an old newspaper. We might find information about the terrible day that Popp has forgotten."

That night, Ola climbed into the library through a high window. The other children waited outside. Two robot guards were inside, so she had to move quietly. She found some boxes of old newspapers. Then she heard a strange noise – "glug glug, gurgle glug."

"That's the sound of drinking," Ola thought. "Who is it? Robots don't drink. How strange!"

At last Ola found the right box. She pulled out some newspapers and was about to leave, when a robot saw her. She dropped one of the papers, but picked it up before she ran out of the library.

The robots were following Ola. Their metal fingers looked like knives in the moonlight.

"Run!" Ola shouted to her friends who were waiting.

"Phew! We've escaped! Come and sleep at Popp's house," Tim said to the twins. "We'll look at these newspapers together."

Leo looked at the paper that Ola dropped in the library.

"There's oil on it," he said. "Where's it from? It smells like the oil that Dad puts in his car engine."

"And it's the same color as the mark in Popp's notebook," said Tim.

"Look at the date!" Carla shouted. "Ola, you found the right newspaper!"

The next morning, the children looked at the newspaper again.
On one page was a story that Tim started to read. Popp walked
into the room. He stood quietly and listened.

Environmental Disaster Hits Verdana

Last night dirty black oil arrived on the beaches of Verdana. Where did it come from? No one knows. The oil has polluted rivers and lakes. Scientists are working hard to make clean water from air.

Tim turned to his grandfather.

"Do you remember now, Popp?" he asked.

"Yes, I do, I do! And I'm sure that the robots brought the oil!"
said Popp.

"I'm scared," said Ola. "The robot guards are looking for us."

"Yes," said Popp. "They know that you stole newspapers from the library. You should hide in the Lost Wilderness. You'll be safe there."

"The Lost Wilderness? What's that?" asked Tim.

"It's a beautiful forest in a valley a long way from here," Popp replied. "I don't know if it's still there. It's called the Lost Wilderness because it's almost impossible to find."

"Do you know the way?" asked Tim.

"No, I've forgotten," Popp replied.

"Let's look in your notebooks for clues," said Ola. "What is this flower, Popp?"

"It's an amazing plant with great powers," Popp replied. "I found it in the underground caves near the entrance to the Lost Wilderness. Then I heard the sound of robots. I had to escape. I dropped my notebook in some oil when I was running away."

"Tell us more later, Popp," said Ola. "We must leave NOW."

"But I don't remember the way," said Popp.

"I've got an idea," said Leo. "The birds will find the forest. They'll see it from above. When they return they'll lead us to the Lost Wilderness through the underground caves."

The little birds flew west over the town, over streets and buildings. They kept on flying, over factories and fields full of big rocks. Rosy saw the green treetops first.

"Hello, goodbye, hello, goodbye," she sang.

The Lost Wilderness lay in a deep valley. Rosy and Bluey flew down to rest in a tree before they returned.

The sun was going down when the birds flew in through an open window.

"They're back! What are they carrying?" Tim asked. He was happy to see them.

"Leaves and flowers!" shouted Popp. "They've found it! They've found the Lost Wilderness!"

"We mustn't lose any more time. The robots are looking for us," said Tim. "We've got to leave immediately." He put flashlights and a blanket in his bag, and Ola put food and drink in hers.

Ola turned to Popp and asked, "Will you be okay, Popp? Are you strong enough?"

Popp waved his walking stick. "I've never been better. Are you ready?" he asked.

"Yes!" they all shouted. "Show us the way Rosy and Bluey!"

So the old explorer, his brave young followers, and two little birds set off on a long and dangerous journey.

It was dark when Popp and the children reached the outside of the city. A long straight road lay ahead, and a cold wind moved over the island.

Tim pointed to some large rocks in a field. "Let's stop there for the night," he said. "It looks like a safe place."

He made a tent between two rocks with the blanket. Then they sat under it and had some dried snacks and water.

"Tell us more about the day of the disaster, Popp. We're not ready to sleep yet," said Carla.

"Sit close and listen carefully," said Popp.

"On my way back to Verdana City I saw oil everywhere," said Popp. "Fish were dying in the rivers, and farm animals were walking on grass that they couldn't eat. I knew that soon nothing was going to grow, and wildlife was going to die. We were lucky to have scientists who could make artificial food, and produce clean drinking water."

"You said that in your opinion the robots brought oil to Verdana," said Carla. "Why did they do that, Popp?"

"I don't know. I guess robots' computers probably went wrong, and then they started acting strangely," said Popp.

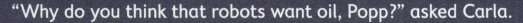

"Why do you think that robots want oil, Popp?" asked Carla.

"Well, perhaps they like to drink it," Popp joked.

"Yes, maybe they think that oil tastes like chocolate!" said Tim.

They all laughed, except Ola. She was thinking about the strange sound in the library – "glug glug, gurgle glug." Was it possible that the robot guards really were drinking oil? Perhaps they did not want anyone to find out because they wanted it all for themselves.

"Robots are not just fierce, dangerous, and horrible – they're also greedy – and I know their secret," Ola thought before she fell asleep.

The next day was bright and sunny. Rosy and Bluey woke Leo first.

"Good morning, good night, good morning!" they sang.

"Hurry up!" said Leo. "It's time to go!"

The travelers walked for many hours. Popp's feet were hurting so he stopped to rest. Suddenly, there was a terrible noise in the sky. Four robots on motorcycles were flying high over the land.

"Hide! Behind that rock!" Ola shouted.

When it was safe to come out, the group walked to another camping place. Popp knew now that the caves were only a few kilometers away.

Next morning, the group quickly reached the caves.

"We're here, thanks to the birds! Turn on your flashlights!" said Popp.

The underground caves were big, and some caves went different ways. Ola shone her flashlight into one, and light fell on thousands of bottles. The writing on them said **Delicious Robot Oil**.

"I've discovered the robots' secret store of oil," she thought, and ran to tell the others. Then she noticed some stalactites on the ceiling of a cave, but forgot to say anything.

Tim was calling "Daylight ahead! I can see trees and sunshine!"

"Three more steps, Popp. You're nearly there," said Tim. He helped his grandfather along the path from the caves into the Lost Wilderness.

They stood and watched the birds in the trees.

"This is the most beautiful place in the world," said Popp sadly. "Or I should say, it *was* the most beautiful place in the world. Do you see that pool over there, children?"

Carla went to look. "It's polluted! There's oil in the water."

Then Ola noticed something hidden behind some rocks. "Look, everyone! A flower! It looks like the flower in Popp's notebook."

The flower was beautiful. It was small, star shaped and bright white. Popp looked at it carefully and said, "What luck! It *is* the flower I drew in my notebook all those years ago. It's called *Lady of the Lake* – isn't that a wonderful name for a flower?"

Popp explained that wise men in the past used this flower to make medicines.

He carefully picked a few leaves and put them in a bowl. He mixed them with water and cooked them over a fire. He then dropped them into the pool. The oil in the lake began to disappear.

"The power of the flower has cleaned the polluted lake. The oil has gone! That's amazing," said Tim.

Popp danced and threw his walking stick in the air. The birds sang and drank from the cool water. The clean water shone silver and blue in the sunlight.

Carla returned to the cave entrance and looked around. Some sunlight shone through a small hole in the roof. "But how did the lake get polluted with oil? We're nowhere near the city or people," she said.

Ola jumped up excitedly and pointed to a dark corner of the cave.

"I was excited, and I forgot to tell you about the secret store," Ola said. "Earlier, I found hundreds of bottles in that cave. They were full of oil. The writing on them said **Delicious Robot Oil**. I think the robots are addicted to the oil and have kept it here."

Popp looked at the bottles and said, "Look, here's a broken bottle, the oil must have polluted the lake. We can't leave these bottles here."

They worked hard together and made a big hole to hide the bottles in. They covered them with rocks. "Done!" said Tim. "Well done!"

"Phew! After all that work I'm really hot,"
said Tim, as he jumped into the cool, fresh lake.

He swam across the water and then shouted out, "Hey, Popp!
There's a river on this side. It looks like it leads out of the Lost
Wilderness."

Popp laughed. "This lake feeds all the rivers on the island,"
he said. "Verdana's water is clean again."

"But we won't have plants," said Tim sadly, "because there
are no seeds in Verdana."

"Yes there are," said Leo. "In the Lost Wilderness."

"We must collect seeds and plants before we go home,"
said Popp.

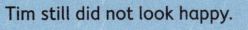

Tim still did not look happy.

"What's the matter, Tim?" Popp asked. "What are you worrying about now?"

"Robots, of course! The water is clean, but the robots are still a problem. They'll be very angry. They'll be even more dangerous when they discover that their oil has disappeared."

"Tim is right," said Carla.

"Yes, he is," said Popp. "We must return home. Back through the caves, and along a secret path around the coast to Verdana City. I know the way."

The group followed Popp through the caves. It was raining when they stepped out into the afternoon light.

Popp knew the way to the coast. The children were nervous because they thought that robots were near.

"Flying machines are noisy," said Popp sensibly. "We'll have time to hide if we hear them."

They sent Bluey and Rosy ahead to look for robots. The birds flew east toward the coast. South of Verdana City, the birds saw something truly amazing. Hundreds of robots were walking along the road to the beach, and hundreds of robots were already in the water. They were moving toward a small pool of oil far out in the ocean.

The birds flew back to Popp and the others. The birds were excited so everyone knew that there was something important to see.

They followed the birds for the rest of that day and through the night. They did not stop to rest.

In the morning, Popp and the children climbed a hill that looked down on a beach. They could hear the sound of people laughing and calling out to each other. Pieces of metal bodies lay on the sand. In the waves out on the ocean, pieces of robot moved gently up and down.

A television presenter and cameras were down on the beach filming the robots.

"The horrible robots have gone! They've gone!" said the presenter to the camera. "We're safe at last."

"Not yet," said Popp wisely. "The robots have gone, but people must change. We must clean up Verdana so animals and plants can live on the island again."

Across Verdana, friends and neighbors worked together to clean up the island. They picked up plastic bags and other garbage in the country, on the beaches, and in the sea. They cleaned the dirty buildings and streets in the towns.

The people dug the hard earth and planted seeds and plants brought from the Lost Wilderness. They watered the land and looked after the plants.

The seasons passed, and fall came. Instead of playing virtual tennis and computer games, the people of Verdana now picked fruit and vegetables and rode horses. Grass grew in the fields, and animals now ate the grass and plants across the island.

Scientists worked hard to find clean ways to make power by using the sun, the wind, and the water.

The people planned a big party on the beach to celebrate.

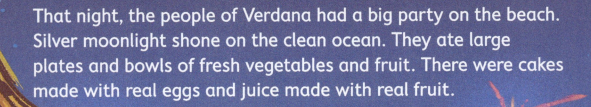

That night, the people of Verdana had a big party on the beach. Silver moonlight shone on the clean ocean. They ate large plates and bowls of fresh vegetables and fruit. There were cakes made with real eggs and juice made with real fruit.

They sang and danced all night, then watched the rising sun.

Popp danced as much as the children. "Aren't you tired, Popp?" asked Tim.

"Not at all!" he replied. "I feel young again, now that I can eat real food and hear the birds sing. I never thought I would see this day," he laughed.

The next day was Monday, and the children went back to school. They had history class first. Leo, Carla, Tim, and Ola gave their history project to Miss King.

Their history project described Verdana before their adventure – the pollution, the frightening robots with their flying motorbikes, the artificial food, and the virtual activities. It described their journey to the Lost Wilderness and their narrow escape from the robots. Popp painted a picture of the Lost Wilderness for their project, too.

The children waited nervously as Miss King looked carefully at the history project.

"This project is very, very late. In fact, it's a whole year late," said Miss King. Then she said brightly, "But it's wonderful! It's the best history project I have ever seen. Well done all of you. We can do so much when we work together."

The children laughed proudly and Carla said, "It's hard to believe so much has changed in one year. Do you still hate history, Leo?"

"No, I love history now!" he replied.

"Wow, I never thought *that* would change!" said Carla.

"And now those horrible robots are history, too!" laughed Tim. "Yippee!"

Before You Read

❶ **Look at the pictures. Think of three words to describe each picture.**

ⓐ 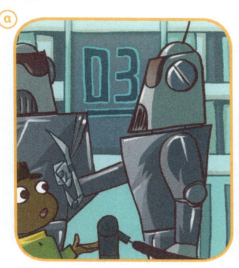 ⓑ

❷ **Find the words below in your dictionary. Then answer the questions.**

> virtual   garbage   seed   disaster   stalactite   polluted

a Can you touch something virtual?

b Is garbage clean or dirty?

c Does a seed come from a plant or a machine?

d Is a disaster something good or something bad?

e Is a stalactite hard or soft?

f Does polluted water help or hurt wildlife?

After You Read

1 **Who in the story …**

a made a tent with a blanket?

b didn't like history?

c climbed through a library window?

d was a plant scientist?

e found the Lost Wilderness?

f went swimming in the lake?

2 **Put the sentences in the order of the story.**

a The special plant cleaned the polluted lake. ☐

b Ola heard the sound of drinking in the library. ☐

c Popp remembered the caves and the Lost Wilderness when the birds sang to him. ☐

d Leo and Carla met Tim and Ola at school. ☐

e The children gave Miss King their history project. ☐

f Ola discovered the robots' store of oil. ☐

g Hundreds of robots were moving toward the ocean. ☐

h Popp and the children walked across the island to the underground caves. ☐

3 **Think of ten adjectives that best describe the Lost Wilderness. Use the words to write about the Lost Wilderness. Then draw a picture of it.**